I Didn't Have A Choice

One Girls story

DAVID LEE HENLEY

Dedication to Anonymous

The Courage to Speak Up. The Will to Survive.
The Ability to Move Forward and Create a New Life.
What More Could be Asked?

DAVID LEE HENLEY

Authors' Note: This is a work of non-fiction. Names and places have been changed to honor the request of anonymity of person giving testimony of actual events. Locales and public names are sometimes used for atmospheric purposes. Any resemblance to real people, living or dead, or businesses, companies, events, institutions, or locales is entirely coincidental.

Any correspondence with the Author can be made through e-mail at:

brutushenley@hotmail.com

CONTENTS

Preface

Before I begin my story, I have a brief comment.

There is a different attitude in society today, which was completely absent when I was growing up. I only wished it had been as it is today back then. Maybe I would then not have had a reason or need to write this book.

People at the time this all happened had an, I don't see, I don't hear, and I don't know anything attitude to things into which they did not want to get involved.

I found as all the horrible things that I had to endure, which were happening to me that everyone who, as I think back upon it, knew what was happening and had simply ignored it so they could justify their inhumanity and cowardice.

Their excuses were as many as the times they encountered me in my need for help. It is none of my business; I don't want to get involved, what difference could I make anyway, all false justification defenses for their lack of common decency and unwarranted and unjustifiable fear.

It has always mystified and frustrated me as to how absolutely everyone for the whole time I was a captive to the person whom I will call a monster in this book that not once did an ounce of help come to me.

Government officials, school officials, hospitals, all believed or accepted the lies told to them. Neighbors, who had to have heard my screams of pain, my family, my own mother; not one would investigate or lift a finger to stop or prevent the suffering and humiliation I had to endure from the monster I had for a step-father.

It has taken me a lifetime to get to the point that I could even attempt to write about this part of my life. It is still excruciating to remember it at all. I feel now that possibly by writing about my experiences, I might save a young girl's life and hopefully get others who know of or suspect these kinds of situations to show some backbone and get involved in stopping the horror.

I have spent years trying to block out the past to no avail. It is and always will be a part of me. I will see or hear something that triggers an instant recall and flashback to that time in life I most want to forget but am unable to. At times it causes panic attacks, of which I have no control, and I think I am having a heart attack.

I wake at night screaming from my nightmares. The monster did his evil on me, and it has left lifelong consequences.

Introduction

Society has always allowed complete changes in its commitments to marriage. Some stay faithful to their promise of unto death oaths even under extraordinary circumstances and situations of suffering. Many have dissolved the union at the first argument. Most run the gauntlet of betweenness.

Others have mostly had beautiful and loving relationships, though they are getting rarer and seen more as in the minority. Most live together just getting along for the children's sake, or that is the excuse of most.

It is not this writer's place to judge any particular set of rules to live by, nor to establish basic living together criteria. Every person designs their very own unique niche in cohabitation with their partner, husband, and wife, significant other, however, you define your arrangement.

There are, however, a few fundamental understandings that are never to be crossed. These are fundamental principles of a civilized society.

Never do harm to your partner and likewise never allow others to harm them. Basic and simple.

There is an understood obligation that from the uniting of couples who bring into the world the consummation of their union, the children, that they also are afforded the same love and care the couple should have for each other.

Therein lies a point where some have crossed that barrier for their own particular selfish wants and desires. It is where sometimes out in the open and sometimes in secret, these rules are cast away.

This is a point where most only do a small thing of little consequence, and from there grows to more severe acts of selfishness and misbehaving. Such possibilities are: by hitting in anger but not truly meaning to, cheating out of a desire for another, and feeling bad about it. Such things are terrible in the scope of things to healthy relationships.

But then you begin to get into more and more outrageous behavior, even unto murder at the extreme. Yes, people can run to extremes of mammoth proportions in their search for self-gratification.

The one thing that even the evilest minded among us do not tolerate is the willful harming of the most vulnerable, the most innocent, the children.

You can prove that point any time by putting someone who willfully and with malice harmed a child into the ranks of the most ardent of criminals, and though they will tolerate each other among themselves, they will kill the molester without a second's hesitation.

It is something inherent in the more significant majority of us to protect the young.

This story is about a girl who was passed over in that protection. She was somehow never given the most basic of protections from all around her. To this day, it is not fully understood how this could have happened to this extent. But happen it did.

It is why this story has to be shared. To help in any way it can by hopefully getting others to stop helping continue this cycle of abuse and to end these horrific situations which are still going on somewhere and are known by others too afraid to speak out.

It must be in this enlightened and courageous time the abused come forward and tell their darkest secrets, which until now were kept buried within families as a shameful thing not to be opened to the light of day. We have to get people out of their comfort zones and speak out if suspicious of some egregious act which might be happening around them, to save the children.

This story is but one story, her story, exclusively unique to her, but its representation is repeated in too many other stories.

It is not this writer's desire to put into words the feelings of horror and suffering that would be inherently and profoundly lived and felt by the storyteller herself. She has had a challenging time in relaying the story to me as it is.

I cannot even guess as a male the emotions and trauma a female must feel at the time of being accosted. I can only give the verbal accounting given to me by the victim.

It will be the reader who must fill in that portion as only a female can. If you're a male reader, maybe a small fraction of the real horrors can be revealed and empathized with from her story.

I give her a grateful thank you for her courage to come forward and expose the man who caused so much harm and try and prevent others from being victimized with the same fate as herself.

I also want to say how much she should be admired for the inner strength she must have to come out of all the horror with her sanity still intact.

Chapter One:

How It All Began

I have found from listening to other women who have gone through the horrors of abuse that no story is the same. Each circumstance was predictably on the same path, but how it happens is unique in each situation.

The bottom line is that once the man decides he is going to do the molesting, it is only a matter of time and opportunity before he acts on his inappropriate, disastrous, shameful, and painful to his victim's lusts.

Nothing is more harmful to a young girl who has given her trust to someone who violates that trust so abhorrently.

Nothing scars deeper the faith one has in finding the most trusted to be so utterly devoid of respect and caring; and be so barren of compassion and concern for the pain and humiliation of putting someone through such a horrific experience.

One that has endured these acts can never again fully feel safe in a man's company. Doubt will always linger in the back of their mind.

One example of this was when I was newly married, and my husband was getting a little too aggressive. It caused me to recoil in fear and spoiled the moment, even though I knew it was not meant in a harsh and insensitive way.

Just the force used in complete ignorance and playful fun by your loved one instigates past repressed feelings and brings them back to life.

This occasion happened only once with my husband, who was pretending to overpower me playfully. I just froze and began crying. He was shocked when he saw I was crying. He could not have known how such a simple thing would so adversely affect me. Honestly, I didn't either until it happened. I thought I had progressed past those moments. He never played that game again.

I think it took a lot out of our relationship in that there are times a woman wants a man to dominate her and not always have to tell them it's okay. That, of course, would be just one more thing the monster has taken from me.

My story should start somewhere, so, I think a point when I was simply another little girl growing up should be appropriate.

Before the monster came into our lives, we, as very young children, used to have a fun time. Mom would date some guys, and they were nice men. We always had fun with them and enjoyed their company. I was about four or five at the time.

Mom was hardly ever around. We stayed with baby sitters most of the time. I suppose she was trying to find a husband to take care of us.

Mom eventually started taking us to see the monster in some prison. It was a long drive. To this day, I will never understand why my mother would want to have anything to do with a man in prison. We would play on the floor while she would talk to the monster through a glass wall. I never knew how mom had gotten to know him. Did she even know why he was there? I never found that out.

We didn't know anything as young children. He treated us pleasantly as he was courting mom. I remember he was always kind to me back then, at first.

He always wanted me around but did not seem to want my brothers around. I remember him starting to get mad at my brothers a lot, and I wondered why he was acting that way toward my brothers; they weren't doing anything wrong.

I think I was about five and a half when mom married him. We children never really liked him. We wished mom would have married one of the other men who were genuinely respectable to us.

There were several verbal fights between mom and grandma. I don't think grandma liked the monster any more than us kids. We were too young to know what it was all about. Mom and grandma never got along very well.

My grandparents told mom to watch out for me around the monster. So obviously they could see something was going on or knew more about the monster than we were allowed to know. I wished they had cared enough to help me more than they did. Mom just dismissed it as them not liking the monster.

It seemed when the monster would talk to my brothers, it was always in a derisory voice, and he would speak to me in a friendly voice.

Mom was never nice to me. I never got hugs from her, and when she combed my hair, it was like she was trying to pull my hair out. I think back on it now, and I think she learned to be uncaring from her mom, my grandma. Or maybe it was an inherited character flaw through her genes. Both were cold, demanding women. Not much love flowed in the family from the women toward the women. Mom always told me I should have been a boy.

She was relentless in her disparaging remarks.

The monster picked the perfect woman to marry for his needs. A woman that was desperate for a man willing to care for her and her kids. A woman who unmistakably wasn't particularly fond of her own flesh and blood daughter. He could no doubt see the similarity of my mother and my grandmother in that they both were alike in their lack of caring, the perfect situation for a manipulating molester to find.

I always thought I should have a mother who would love and protect me, but she never hugged me or said she loved me. She just told me I should have been a boy.

I always had fantasies about my father. I would be daddy's little girl. That was a fantasy in any little girls' dreams. It just didn't work out that way.

I remember mom married the monster in our grandparent's living room.

He could now start his slow and methodical power and control over everyone as he had always done to everyone around him to the point of blind obedience to his will. Making everyone scared to death of him seemed to be his goal.

When I was six or seven, things started getting worse. Mom was working days at a hospital, so she was never around when the monster mistreated us. That gave the monster a couple of years to work on my brothers and me, but especially on me as I would soon be cast as the only one able to stop him from hurting my brothers. That was the threat he would eventually come to use.

She would come home from work, and my brothers would tell her the monster was mistreating us, but she didn't ever do anything about it. She just said we must have been doing something wrong and probably deserved to have been punished for it. She just shrugged it off.

Chapter Two:

The Monster Is Here

Finally, the day came as it inevitably would, the day he could no longer wait to satisfy his lust for little girls.

I was in the third grade when one day he told me he was going to pick me up at lunchtime so I could go home to eat. I can still remember that day as clear as a bell. I must have been nine years old then, although I seem to feel I was more like seven and a half or eight years old.

I thought that was strange and puzzling of him wanting to take me home for lunch, but I was not feeling very well that day, so I did what I was told. He took me home and fixed me a sandwich.

After I ate it, he told me to go take a bath. That was really surprising and unexpected. I wondered why he wanted me to take a bath. But he was harsh to me then, and I was too scared to say no. So, I went and took a bath. Then he came into the bathroom, and I told him to get out. He just came in and sat down on the tub rim. He told me he was going to do some things to me. I wondered, of course, what things he was talking about. He said to me if I told my brothers or my mother anything, he would hurt my brothers really badly.

Well, I loved my brothers. I told him, I didn't want him to hurt my brothers, I don't like you hurting my brothers.

He said, then don't tell anybody about what I am going to do. That is when I started crying. Back then, you always did what your parents tell you to do, no matter what.

I didn't even know what he was going to do, but I knew I wasn't going to like it. I didn't want him in the bathroom, and I couldn't figure out why he would come in there anyway. I was embarrassed by him being there, and seeing me naked and unable to do anything about it was more than I could handle.

All I could do was cry and tell him to stop as he forced himself on me. I tried fighting him, but it was useless. He was too big and strong. He just kept telling me to be quiet and to stop crying.

I don't want to tell all the obvious things he did to me in the tub and later after he made me go to the bedroom. It is hard enough to even talk about it now. But, as I was too small for him then, he continued day after day, month after month until I could finally take him inside me. He made me do more and more things for him.

I can never forget the horrible pain and humiliation of those times.

I am sure the neighbors could hear me screaming and crying out in pain. But no help ever came.

Months went by. I was missing school so often now because the monster took me home almost every lunch period, and the truant's officers were starting to come around asking questions. I would have to re-take the third grade because of the missed time. That was when we suddenly moved to the south.

It was my grandparents that loaned the monster the money to move to the south when the school started calling at our house about me missing so much time. Mom had lied to them about the reason they needed the money. She said she needed the money to buy a house, but it was money needed to run away from the prying eyes coming around looking into my absence from school.

The monster simply could not stop himself from taking me out of school for his pleasures. Once he started on me, he could not stop, even to help himself stay out of jail. He was indeed one sick monster. So, we ran or moved away as it were.

Thinking back on that time, I think the only reason we would have suddenly moved was to save the monster from the prying eyes of the state looking into what was going on. I just wished they would have followed up on their investigation instead of dismissing it as, oh well, not our problem any longer. Mark up another failure by the government to do its job.

The first house we moved to was remote, deep in the woods, and it had all the privacy the monster could need. It didn't have anything but a roof. We had to use an outside toilet and take bathes in a metal tub. All us kids hated it.

Now the monster could have me anytime he wanted with no problems.

As I look back now, I had thought my mom was supposed to be there for me, to be my friend, but she never was. She never cared to help me with my homework; she never cared if it was even done. She only cared if I didn't finish the chores. She was never there most of the time anyway. She was always working.

The monster got hurt doing some job and was electrocuted. He stayed in the hospital for a while. That was before my half-sister was born, I think.

When the monster got out of the hospital, things got really bad then.

Time seemed to stop then. I just lived from one day to the next, always at his side. He made sure I could never have a moment alone with anyone that I could confide in, just in case I tried to get help. But he had worked on me very well. I was totally under his control and did not even think of trying anything. I did what I knew I had to do to keep my brothers as safe as possible.

Once the monster came into our lives, my brothers and I lost a lot of our playtime together. It was always chores and angry confrontations. The monster was always on us about something, anything to keep us under his rule.

Even as I did everything demanded of me, it seemed he would still hurt my brothers. There was just no way around it.

Later in life, I remember when I finally did tell my brothers about what happened to me. They just started yelling at me. Why didn't you tell us? Why did you put up with all that from him for so long?

Everything is always my fault. I get the blame for everything that happens. I can understand how they felt and why they were so upset, but I had no control over anything. I did what I had to do.

It really hurt me to have them yelling at me. I couldn't answer a lot of their questions; I just froze up from all the verbal yelling coming at me. I was sorry I had even told them.

Now everyone was mad at me. I thought I would get a little sympathy and understanding, but all I got was anger. I never thought I would be viewed as the bad one for trying to keep them all safe from the monster.

I withdrew back into my shell again. Their hatred for the monster just went up ten-fold, but without my keeping them safe by doing what I did, they may not have even been there today. It was now my burden to bear alone.

When the monster opened up an antique sales and refurbishing business, I would go everywhere with him. We would travel to distant locations and always sleep in the truck.

I was allowed to only work in the back, or if customers came in, I would have to stand at his side. He had such a tight rein on me. I would just look at the ground while he talked to the customers. I could tell everyone thought it was strange how I acted, but they never said anything.

This was the south. I think a lot was going on in other homes as was in mine, and people just turned a blind eye to it. A don't get involved attitude.

Of course, there was no place he would not have me when he felt like it, even at the business.

I did get to go fishing with him. I loved fishing. It was the only fun I can remember having. Of course, I knew it was just another reason to get me away from the house for his pleasures, but by then, it was just a chore to me. I came to expect it as something that was going to happen, so I concentrated on the positive parts, like my love of fishing. I at least managed to find some fleeting moments to treasure.

I never felt any of the pleasure people claimed to have from sex. I suppose I had blocked out any feeling to it like a normal person. My body was dead to any senses. I just went through the motions as he would ask of me. If there were any time I had felt the sensual side of the act, I must have blocked it out. My mind would never allow such things.

Later I will tell of my eventual awakening to the feeling of pleasure, but it was never once with the monster. The monster never thought of making me feel good. I was only around for his enjoyment, his gratification.

After my oldest brother got dad to let him come live with him, it was just my younger brother, and I left to suffer the monsters' wrath. I was glad at least one of us was able to escape. I used to wonder why dad would not take all of us away from this constant terrorizing by the monster. I was sure my brother would tell him how bad it was for us here. But I guess it was not a concern of his.

Of course, my half-sister was there, but she was the monsters' little darling and was spoiled rotten. It was my job to see to her every want and need.

As a punishment for not doing what the monster wanted, he would send my younger brother to bed and lock him in, as usual, to make me more cooperative to his wishes.

I remember I begged the monster to feed my brother before he was locked in his room at night.

It was just another torture he inflicted on him to make sure I did what he wanted. He had to pee out the window because he could not go to the bathroom, locked up as he was.

It made me feel so bad for him. I knew I would be responsible for anything that happened to my brother if I did not put out for the monster. I always tried hard not to go to sleep until my half-sister went to sleep, and I could go to his bedroom to satisfy his needs.

Mom would never stick up for the boys when the monster would hurt or mistreat them.

The day my last brother, the youngest, left to go live with our father, he had gotten into a fistfight with the monster. He was older now, and he would not take any more beatings from the monster. He beat him up pretty good. The monster was backing up from the fists coming at him and tripped over something. When he went down, my brother got on top of him and pounded him good. But the monster got up and was saying he was going to kill my brother. I yelled for my brother to run. The monster was going into the house to get the shotgun. I knew he meant to kill my brother.

My brother waited in the gulley by the road until mom came home. The monster was sitting on the porch for my brother to come back. He stopped her and told her what had happened.

I was sorry then that I had not poisoned him on the many times I dreamed of doing it. I always did the cooking, so my fantasy was putting poison in his food, but I never acted on it. I don't know if I could have anyway. The fear of failing and his surviving kept me from trying. I think it was also that I am not a murderer even to save my own life; it didn't stop me from thinking about it, though.

My brother had run to save his life, and eventually when mom came home, and she got the monster to agree to send my brother away to his father to live, that saved his life. I was so happy that both of my brothers were now free from the monster.

Mom would have horrible fights with the monster. Then she would tell me we would leave him after my half-sister was older. I would beg her to leave him now, but she never did. She never left him, ever.

I could never figure out why my father did not ask for me to come live with him. Of course, thinking about it, he never asked for any of us. The boys had been forced back on him. My oldest brother had constant arguments with the monster, and mom finally sent him to live with dad.

My brothers I am sure had told of all the horrors the monster had put us through, except of course the part about the secret only the monster and I knew.

I used to wonder why dad had not thought to ask for me to be also sent? Never once did I hear from him. No letters, phone calls, nothing, it was only later when I finally was able to talk to him that it came out. He never wanted a daughter, just boys. I can't tell you how much that hurt. It was like stabbing me in the heart. I wished I had never asked him.

My brothers had been sent away to live with our birth father before my first pregnancy, so they never knew what was going on. If they had been there at that time and found out what had been going on, I could not say if any of us would be here today. I think the monster would very quickly and with no guilt have killed us to protect himself from prosecution.

The prophylactics he used were always breaking, and it caused me to become pregnant twice by him in the time I was there.

The most heartbreaking thing I can remember was coming home from school one day and finding our home had burned down.

We were having trouble with a leaking hot water tank, and the reason given as to why the house burned down was because it had lost all the water and exploded. The house was so old, and the wood so dry, it just burned too fast for anyone to stop. It was gone before anyone could even get to it. Every one of the few things I had was gone. I had nothing left but the clothes I had on. I just cried and cried.

We had some neighbors that let us sleep on their screened-in porch until we could rebuild the house, but as it was rebuilt on the old foundation, it always smelled of burned wood, a constant reminder of my loss.

As I said earlier, I was never allowed to have friends. I never even got to play with my brothers. I had to take care of my half-sister. She did get to have her friends over to play and was allowed to go to their house as well. The monster would take me to the shop and leave my half-sister with mom.

As I said earlier, once mom had found out about us, she never stopped him from doing anything with me. I was his to do with as he pleased.

I remember when I was older, my oldest brother, who I hadn't seen in years came to visit with his wife. He finally got a moment alone with me and asked me if I wanted to leave with him. I was shocked, and in response, I told him I had to stay and take care of my half-sister.

It was so sudden and so unexpected I didn't have time to think about it. I was so sad when he left, and I was back to my old life again. I regularly cried, outwardly, and inside. I sometimes wonder if he had been more determined and persistent in getting me to go if I would have gone.

Mental chains are harder to break than steel ones.

After my brother left, the monster told me to quit crying, slut. He always called me that. The monster and mom both would call me that in front of everybody. I was a slut in mom's eyes, and I was a slut in his eyes.

People would just stare at him and look at me. But again, no one helped me, ever. It was so embarrassing. I didn't want the public to look at me in that way.

Here I was trying to protect my half-sister or thinking I was at the time. I found out later after I left, he started doing her as well. She was twelve years old. I had thought she would be safe because she was his little darling.

I always tried to find a way to escape, but the monster was continuously close by. I couldn't even go to town. I never went to town with mom. She didn't want me around her.

I don't know how I made it to the eighth grade. I was always failing everything. I had no help. I didn't have time to do my homework or study. I would start my day by waking before anyone, and cooking breakfast for everyone, then doing the dishes, getting my half-sister ready for school, then I could think of getting myself prepared to go to school.

Mom had gotten a job in town working in a retirement home and got home after midnight, so it gave the monster all the time he wanted with me at night. I was left to do all the work around the house myself.

When I came home from school, I had to clean the house, milk the cow, churn and strain the butter from the milk, take care of my half-sister, cook for everybody, do the dishes, wash the clothes, clean the barn, pick up the cow droppings, do the gardening.

Of course, those were just a few of the chores I had to do. As the tasks were needed, I did them until they were all done. Then I had to wait till I could service the drunken monster before I could sleep.

Many times, my half-sister would wake up when I tried to slip out of bed to go to the monster, and I would tell her to go back to sleep, and I needed to wait till she was asleep. The longer I took, the drunker he became, and that made my job a lot harder.

Many times, she would wet the bed, and I would have to get up and change my clothes, and hers, and the bed, before she would finally get to sleep. This was my life.

I never had a mother who talked to me about anything. I was never told about a period, and when I started, I was so scared. I thought I was broken somehow inside.

I wrote to my father about three times, begging him to come and get me. I never got an answer. I found out later that he never received them. I finally figured out the monster had checked the mailbox and took the letters. I didn't think about the possibility he would take them. I was so naive.

As I think back on it now, I realize the monster must have taken my letters because he would tell me my father didn't want me, he never writes you, he doesn't care about you. I think if my father did write to me, the monster would have destroyed them as well. He did have absolute control of me.

I will say, the only truth the monster told me was that my dad really didn't want me. I will hurt from that truth until I am dead.

I had asked my mom to send me to dad's, but she never had the money for that. My dad had been a policeman, and I wondered why he never wanted to know how I was doing. It probably would not have mattered anyway. My father told me later that he never wanted me in his life. He never wanted a daughter.

No one wanted me. I was all alone in the world. I wondered many times why I should keep on living. This was no life. I was reaching my breaking point.

There came a time I guess the last one or two years I was there. I would see the public from the back of the antique store staring at me. I was so big and old. At least that is how I thought of myself. Girls my age were usually married, and I was so fat and homely because of how I was made to dress and cut my hair. I was still forced to use the bowl on my head to cut my hair above the ears.

I would stand around the shop just waiting for the monster to tell me what to do. I was getting older now and finally starting to realize just how controlled I was. I had to go to the people's houses to do work on antiques, and I saw the way the people would stare at me and ask me why am I still at home? How old are you? Don't you work? I would have to go into these people's homes and strip the furniture and cabinets, and they would just stare at me, wondering why I was doing all of this. I was older now, and everyone knew the monster was married to my mother.

It was apparent now to them what was going on. At those times right in front of all those people, he would call me a little bitch or you little slut, or whore. I didn't know what those words meant except I knew they hurt. I was so embarrassed.

I started thinking, is life really so bad out there that I need to stay here putting up with this. Could there be anyone out there that might want me? There's got to be someone out there that wants me. I just could not do this any longer. I could not keep living like this. I would either find a way to escape or die trying; I was done. I had reached my breaking point.

Even the times when I got sick, I had to go to work at the shop or do my chores at home. The monster never gave me any sympathy. I would sit there, stripping furniture and throw up. It didn't matter to him.

For a year and a half before I left, I felt a lump in my breast, like a golf ball. I told mom I had a lump, and she asked me how long I had it. I told her a year and a half. She put me in the hospital where the doctors removed my nipple and took out the lump and put back my nipple. I was fine after that.

Chapter Three:

The Escape

I became so sick one day. I was throwing up frequently and had a high temperature. I could not get out of bed. So, the monster, for the first time in my life, left me alone at the house. I suppose he thought I was too sick to try anything.

I don't know why I did it, but I remembered where the monster kept a jar of money under the sink. For the first time in my life, I was alone without the monster around. I was scared to death. I was twelve miles out of town with no way to get there, and I was sick as a dog.

I had never been out in public alone.

Imagine if you were put into a room and not allowed out for sixteen years, that was what it was like. I never got out of the chamber of horrors. I was twenty-four years old. It was time to do this or die trying.

I knew the monster's parents lived 7 miles away. They knew what was going on with me by this time, I am sure.

I called them up and told them I have to do this. I have to do it now. Would you please drive me to the bus station? I was so petrified they would say no because they were afraid of the monster as well, but they were my only chance of escape.

I was to the point that I said to myself, I am going to either kill myself, or I will just do this. What did I have to lose? There was a gun in the house to end it all and a jar of money under the sink. I chose the money. I told myself I have been used and humiliated long enough.

This world cannot be as bad as the monster has told me it was. If it is, someone can just come and kill me if it was.

So, what I did was, I got under the sink and took $288.00. I was more scared than I had ever been in my life. I thought the monster would drive up at any moment. He had the truck, so I reasoned, or more like hoped, he thought it was okay to leave me sick at home.

I remember one time he had an argument with his parents, and he called his mom a bitch and his father a bastard and told them he hoped they burned in hell.

I called up his parents and talked to his mother.

I said, "I am all alone. I stole $288.00. Could you please come and take me to the bus station?"

She said, "I will be right there." She immediately hung up.

What wonderful people. It was like they were just waiting for me to ask for their help. I thought, had it always been just that simple. Just ask?

True to her word, they were there in minutes. I was so afraid when I saw them because they had to go by the shop where the monster was to get to the house. I was scared he would be right behind them.

I had earlier called the greyhound bus station and asked them if they had a bus that went nonstop to Huntington Beach, California?

They said, "we have a bus that was going to leave here at three o'clock."

I threw a few clothes into a little suitcase. I was scared, I was shaking, and adding to all of that, I was sick as a dog.

I watched for the monster's parents, and when they came, I ran out and jumped in their car.

I said, "would you please hurry? If the monster knows!"

Before I could finish my statement, she said, "honey, I know."

I said, "would you please hurry? Just get me on the bus."

Okay, here I was, having never been to town alone before, running as fast as I could toward the cliff of freedom. Just take the leap, I was persuading myself. As I grabbed the ticket, I was thinking, oh God, please don't let the monster come and get me. I was wondering if he had come home yet?

Well, they left me at the bus station. It cost me $110.00 for the one-way ticket. I got on the bus, and I was panicking and crying. The bus driver looked at me, but I was afraid of the bus driver too. I said again to myself; I've got to do this. I have got to do this if it kills me. At least I can say I went, I tried.

The bus finally left the depot. It seemed like it was never going to depart. I was crazy with panic, worry, and dread.

I think about that moment, and it reminded me of a movie I once saw. It was a man that had jumped from an airplane, and his parachute did not open properly, and he was falling to certain death.

His only recourse was to cut the lines from the malfunctioning parachute and deploy the reserve parachute before he hit the ground and died.

That few moments, he was working to save his life was exactly where my mind was when I decided to run. Time was not on his or my side. Both scenarios were life or death, and it was our moment to succeed or fail. Live or die. I believe the emotions were the same as well.

The first place we stopped was in Memphis, Tennessee.

I asked the bus driver if he could help me. " I need to get to Huntington Beach, California."

The bus driver said, "I tell you what, you stay on this bus, and if you need to get off to get something to eat or use the bathroom, you have twenty-five minutes before we leave."

I didn't know then we had bathrooms in the back of the bus. I would be too afraid to walk past all those people anyway. I sat in the seat behind the driver. I suppose for whatever security that would be, and I could make sure he didn't leave without me.

I was so afraid to get off the bus at that time. I was fearful it might leave without me. But eventually, I got famished and needed to go to the bathroom, so I left just long enough to go to the bathroom.

On the way back from the bathroom, I saw a food concession stand. It was selling sandwiches. I asked the girl how much a sandwich was, and she said something close to $2.00. She asked me if I wanted one and I said, no thank you.

I didn't know how far it was to California and how much it would cost me to eat on the way. I was used to sandwiches I made at home with a big slice of bologna. This thing looked like you could see through it.

I went back to the bus, and the next stop on the journey, the driver said we would be there for thirty minutes. I saw him going to a restaurant. I thought, well, I would follow him, I could be sure not to miss the bus. The bus driver noticed I was following him and asked me again if I was okay.

He said, "I noticed you have been crying most of the trip."

I told him I was fine.

He said, "well, okay. I am going in here to eat."

I uttered it! "You are?"

So, I went in and watched him just to be sure he didn't leave without me.

The waitress came over and asked me what I wanted. She gave me the menu, and I looked at it. The prices were three to four dollars for sandwiches with chips. I was used to eating big meals, and I finally ordered a hamburger. I ate it so fast. I was starved to death.

So, I rode the bus for three days and two nights. I was thinking, was I ever going to make it to Huntington Beach? There was a point in Los Angeles where I had to change buses. So, I went to the counter and asked the girl there; I am supposed to change buses to get to Huntington Beach, can you help me?

She said sure. Take bus 86 it is leaving in about twenty-five minutes.

I freaked out, twenty-five minutes? I asked her quickly, twenty-five minutes? Where do I go to catch it? She told me, and I went to the bus. I usually sat in the second seat, but I didn't want the driver to see me. I was having a hard time controlling my fear and crying.

Luckily, I had sat alone all across the country. Or maybe it was because people just didn't want to be bothered or get involved with a crying young girl.

When I had gotten into L.A., I saw people sleeping in the bus terminal, wearing dirty clothes, talking to themselves. I saw women wearing weird clothes. I didn't know what to think. It scared me.

I went to the bathroom and said to myself, hurry up, you need to get out of here. It stunk so bad. I straddled the toilet. I wasn't going to sit on that nasty seat for anything, and I had to pay ten cents to get into the toilet.

When I finally got to Huntington Beach, there was a little place called Terry's cafe. I decided that it would be better than staying in the terminal.

So, I went in, sat down, and said to myself; I have to get my strength up.

I had my younger brother's old phone number. I didn't even know if it still worked, but I had to wait till he got off work to call it.

When he finally answered the phone, I said: "Hello Paul, this is your sister Janet, I am in Huntington Beach, and I am trying to find dad, do you know where he is?"

He yelled, "Janet, did you say you're in Huntington Beach, California?"

I said, "yes."

I questioned him again. "Come on, Paul, where is dad?"

He said, "he is right around the corner."

He gave me dad's number.

I called, and dad could not believe it was me.

He said, "where are you?"

I said, "I am in this little Terry's cafe Paul said was right around the corner from you, but I don't know how to find you."

He said, "you stay right there."

I said, "Okay."

So, I walked out in front of the restaurant, and down the street, I saw walking on the sidewalk, my oldest brother Jim, my dad, and his wife.

I had not seen my dad since I was a little girl.

But when he rounded the corner, I started crying. I said to myself; I know that is my dad. I am thinking, Oh My God, this is actually happening. My life-long dream was now a reality.

They came up to me, and dad hugged me, his wife said hi, and also hugged me.

My brother Jim said, "Damn Janet, you're really here," as he also gave me a huge bear hug.

We walked back over to where dad worked, and he went back to his job, and I talked to my brother Jim until it was time to go home. We went to dad's house, and we talked and got to know each other.

I stayed for a week. Then dad asked me where all my clothes were.

I said, "this is all I have. It is all I brought in my little suitcase, two pairs of pants and a shirt. That's all I could take. All my clothes and stuff are still back home. I just need to go get them."

I couldn't ask him to buy me any clothes. I wasn't going to ask him to buy me new things. I didn't know how his wife was. I know she raised the boys Now she's got me?

My brothers used to tell me how they hated her. I wondered if she would even accept me being here.

I stayed that whole week, and I told dad, "I hate to tell you this, but I need to fly back and get my clothes and stuff."

He stated, "I thought you didn't want to go back."

I said, "I don't have anything. I don't have any clothes. I don't have but one pair of shoes and a couple of changes of clothes. What am I going to do? What else can I do?"

He said, "Okay."

Here he is not offering to buy me any clothes. I had thought when I got out to California; dad would buy me clothes. He raised the boys and made sure they had clothes, surely, he'll take care of me.

Well, he wouldn't. That kind of shocked me. But I didn't know how to ask him for help. I didn't want to have to ask him. He didn't want me anyway; I was always told. What was I supposed to do?

He said, "are you really going back?"

I was devastated. I had no choice if my dad wasn't going to help me.

I told him I needed $300.00.

He gave me $300.00 for a round trip ticket.

I flew back to get my stuff, and the flight back would be the next day.

I still don't know how I was able to do it. I was stuck with no alternative.

I called mom, she met me at the airport and brought me back home.

Well, the monster begged me to stay, promising to get me my own apartment. Then the monster started crying. I could not believe it. The monster was crying!

I told him, "I only came to get my clothes, and I am leaving."

He said, "oh, you're not leaving; you're staying."

I mustered every ounce of courage I could.

I said, "look, I only came to get my clothes, and I am leaving."

He started crying again and said, "I kind of figured for the last two years you were going to leave."

I said, "you're married to my mother, okay? My mother doesn't want me here."

I said, "I can't stay here; I have to go."

I could not believe this was happening.

He said, "well, I'll get you an apartment."

I said, "I have to go tomorrow, and I am packing."

I went upstairs and was scared to death. It took every ounce of courage I could muster to show them I meant to do precisely as I said I was going to do.

I took two trunks upstairs and started packing. I packed everything I could. I didn't know if the monster would even allow me to leave.

I had walked back into the prison, but I didn't think I had a choice. Dad was of no help. I had to do this all alone, as usual. But this time, I had my brothers who knew where I was and would come if I didn't make it back.

I think the monster knew it also, and the jig was up for him. He didn't have a choice now. He didn't know how much I had shared with everyone about him. He was gambling I would not tell and keep him out of jail. But that didn't stop him from trying to get me to stay. Control is hard to give up, I supposed.

I didn't know at the time dad and his wife didn't want me there, but it was the only place I had to go then, even if I had forced my way onto him, and after all, he was my dad.

The monster kept crying. I didn't sleep all night. I could not believe he had cried. Wet tears were clearly running down his face. Mom started crying, and my half-sister started crying. They all started crying. I could not believe it. They all treated me like mud on their shoes or worse, now they are crying like little babies.

The next morning, I told my mother to take me to the airport now. Take me now.

Come to find out when I had gotten to dad's house; there was a letter there from the monster telling me he had gone to all the bus stations in a hundred-mile radius of the house looking for me. I had made it to the bus station and left just before he got there. If he had gone to Memphis, he probably would have caught up with me. Lucky for me, he went to all the other stations hoping I was still there waiting to board.

The monster somehow found out his parents had taken me, and he didn't speak to them for years afterward.

I am pretty sure that it didn't bother them in the least. It was probably a blessing from God for helping me escape.

They took me to the airport, and I flew back to dad's house. When he picked me up at the airport, I pinched myself and said I couldn't believe it. I did it. I'm actually gone for good. I got out of prison.

I never spoke to my mother ever again. I don't know the proper way to prepare it, but verbally I disowned her.

She was never to exist as a part of my life again.

Chapter Four:

What Will I Do Now?

I now had to deal with my dad and his wife. No matter what, I did exactly what his wife told me to do. I still had stitches in my breast from the lump I had removed. I stayed with dad for about a month, and he would take me over to the jewelry store he owned. I asked him if he wanted me to sweep the floor for him. He said no.

I look back now and think he just took me along to get me away from my stepmother.

I was so naive, and they saw that. After all, I had an eighth-grade education at best. I never stepped out in public alone in my life; I had zero communication skills; I knew nothing about anything. They were sophisticated, upper-class high society. I was simply an embarrassment to them. A fat unladylike country bumpkin with a bowl haircut. How could I possibly fit into their cultured lives?

Dad's wife was getting jealous. She did not like me there, taking time from her husband.

I finally said I needed to get a job. Dad thought that was a good idea. It would get me out of the house and hopefully out of their lives. Well, not out of their lives but out from under-foot.

My dad worked in jewelry. He sold and gave appraisals to a vast clientele. He gave a party one night at his home, and not knowing what to do with me; he put some of his jewelry on me to show off to his guests. I was told just to be quiet and show the jewelry. But that was a disaster. I was an embarrassment all night. An overweight backwoods country girl with no societal skills, with a bowl haircut? The daughter of the host? That would never happen again.

Dad suggested I try the fast-food restaurant a mile and a half down the road in seeking a job. I walked down to it as no one would drive me there.

I went in and asked for the manager. I told him I needed a job badly. I told him I had never had a job before, but I did work refurbishing antiques for years. I said I didn't know how even to make a hamburger. I thought that was dumb to say as I really did know how but just not the way they did it in the restaurant.

He looked at me and said, you know what? I am going to hire you. I have a bunch of people here that feel like they can call in sick every time a good beach day shows up and leave me without a complete crew. I don't see you doing that. I am going to give you a chance. Also, I can train you the way I want things done without having to break any bad habits you might have learned elsewhere.

Three months later, I was made assistant manager over all the other employees who didn't like that one bit. One of them told me he had been there for a year, and he felt he should have gotten that position.

I told him he needed to talk to the manager, not me. He was the one that gave the job to me.

He didn't talk to the manager. I needed only to be taught one time, mostly on how to do something, and that was it. I took the job very seriously. I wanted to prove to everyone I could be needed and wanted. I was not going to bow down to any threats or misdirected attitudes from anyone ever again.

I was free, and I planned to stay that way.

Dad never did take me to my job or offer to buy me a car, so I saved my first two checks and bought a bicycle to get to work and back.

Eventually, my hair grew out, and I lost my fat from working, walking, and riding the bicycle. I never knew I looked so good. It shocked me to see the woman I had always been under all the deliberate hiding of my beauty the monster had put on me.

I started caring about my appearance, and to have respect for myself. I learned how to dress in beautiful clothes and how to apply makeup to accentuate my face best. I still had a heavy southern accent in my speech, but that just seemed to make me more appealing to the men I met.

After a while, the manager said he wanted to make me the supervisor of my very own restaurant. That petrified me. I had no education to do a position like that, nor had I ever held such responsibility.

I did not have the confidence at that point in my life to even consider it. It was apparent he saw my potential, but I didn't.

I was still just barely free from being a slave, and now I was being asked to take on such a dominant, authoritative position?

My lack of schooling left me at a significant disadvantage, and I knew I was over my head at that time in doing the books required for that position. I could work at any job in the restaurant, but the bookkeeping was out of my comfort zone and my education level.

That offer, I am sorry to say, was too soon in my self-awakening period. I was still too uncertain of myself and my abilities.

It would take a lot longer for me to finally break through my inner-most secret fears of whether people would accept me and find me worthy.

My brainwashing had gone on for seventeen years and would take a lot more achievements and resolve to break that hold, especially without help from anyone.

I would eventually come to realize I had skills, talent, and intelligence, which put me at the top of every job I worked at, but it was certainly not at this time in my life. I was soon to realize some places were male-dominated and was hindered, or should

I say down-right blocked, in getting past a particular position.

But at this time in my life, I was still a fresh new delicate seedling flower just starting to grow after coming out of a terribly difficult winter.

I was still learning what a genuine real life was to be. How wonderful and exciting things happening all around me were. Truly mesmerizing in their moment of reassurance, and comforted me that I had made the right choice to live and escape.

To have freedom, to answer only to myself. To maybe someday share myself with someone I wanted to share with, and who would love me as I would love him!

That man would eventually come into my life. And through him, I was to finally experience my first orgasm. I never knew what it was.

He had me relax and close my eyes. He put my most favorite CD on, and I listened to it with earphones. All I had to do was relax and feel the sensations he was giving me; I had to do nothing fo him, to him, with him. I had nothing to do but immerse myself, my mind, my body, in my own world of music and sensations.

Everyone knows what it feels like to have orgasms. But for me, it was indescribable. I never knew it existed up to that time. I cried from the exquisite pleasure I had never known before; it was so beautiful. From that moment on, I was able to feel the pleasures sex could bring.

It had opened me up mentally and physically, letting in all the senses I had forced down to the bottom-most depths of my being. All the things I would never allow the monster to have me feel were finally open to me.

It was no longer just another chore.

I do not want to spoil this moment, but I have to keep going on my story.

There was a big problem I never saw coming. It was a devastating blow. I had given birth to two children by the monster. My husband and I tried to have a child of our own, but after failing for so long, I finally went to the doctor, and he said I had too much scar tissue in my tubes, and the sperm could not get through to impregnate me. I could have my tubes cleaned out to remove the scar tissue, but that meant I could possibly have a tubular pregnancy. The only way was maybe using in-vitro fertilization. A slim chance back then.

My father would not loan us the money. He said there were too many kids in the world anyway. He was always saying no to me anytime I asked him for help financially. He was wealthy and spent his money on fine things, but tight as they come with me. We could not afford it ourselves, so we just gave up on the idea of ever having children of our own.

My dad died many years later, after having sold a big company and made millions. He never gave us anything except a three-thousand-dollar loan one time, which I paid him back.

He lost his mental faculties, which none in the family knew was happening, and lost or gave away most of his money to unscrupulous people that had surrounded him at that time. He was basically penniless at the end.

I heard he would walk around with a briefcase full of money, just handing it out to whomever he felt.

I was still sad I could not be with him at the end, but he was just too far away, and I could not afford to go to him.

My brother took care of him for all of us.

Dad had called him and asked if he could come and take care of him as he was getting worse health wise and my brother told him he would need to help him financially. Dad said, no problem.

So, my brother left his home and went to take care of dad just to find out he was broke. Dad could not help him because he was broke.

It cost my brother a bankruptcy in the process of doing that for dad. He lost everything he once had, but he still took care of dad until the end.

Sacrifice appears to run in the family, but martyrdom pays a heavy price.

I received word from my brother that mom had called and told him that the monster had died from a massive heart attack while he was doing a sermon at a local church.

I could not believe he had died while preaching. He never set foot in a church in his life. I can only surmise even God had tolerated enough of the monster at that point.

Chapter Five:

It is Great to Be Alive

I have many moments in my story that would eventually define and portray who I have become as a person.

The many girlfriends, a few boyfriends, co-workers in the many varied occupations I have learned.

The skills I have learned that helped me grow, learn and expand my knowledge and abilities.

The moments I treasure most are the times when something new comes along. I can experience a whole new set of joys and laughter and thrills. I have had a lifetime of negativity, and I want only to live the rest of my life looking on the brighter side.

Traveling across the country, I get to see and experience the wonders it has to offer, meeting the people, hearing their stories.

Yes, and also tasting the multitude of flavors from so many diverse cultures and cuisines bursting with their own uniqueness.

I can hardly believe I have been able to do so much. In my darkest hours, I could only imagine such an existence as I now have! I am so thankful I was able to keep from taking my life; to have the chance to become all I ever wanted or dreamed I could be.

I can only imagine who and what I would have become if I had been allowed to live a normal healthy life growing up.

But I am content now at this moment because it is of my precise, with free-will, choosing.

Life now is what I have made of it. It is a manifest reality of my personal creation.

I am going to enjoy it for as long as God allows me.

BIOGRAPHY

David Henley, born in West Memphis, Arkansas, grew up while moving from place to place. He spent three years in Germany in the Army and has worked many jobs starting at age twelve. Such diversity has allowed a great deal of interaction with society and given him many encounters from which to draw life lessons from in his writings.

In his debut book {POEMS, LYRICS AND DIVERSE THOUGHTS}, he imparts a particular moment in time, that everyone can find within themselves which should awaken a memory they have at one time lived. The lyrics in this book are from the songs he has written.

{THE LAST RIDE IS FREE} is his first thriller fantasy novel about three people and their adventures in the world of criminals and honest society. A journey from the dark side of humanity toward a more enlightened soul- searching encounters.

{THE LAST RIDE IS FREE: BOOK TWO} is his continuation of a fantasy thriller novel in a series about the Malone family. It is packed with the same nonstop action as the first book.

It has also brought their son into the fold as an agent working alongside his parents, Mario and Julie.

{THE LAST RIDE IS FREE: BOOK THREE} is the final novel in the series of the Malone Family. It brings the whole family full circle.

As usual, it has many adventures and missions but also has secrets about the family that even they were not aware of all finally brought to fruition.

{A DAY IN THE LIFE OF SARGENT SMITH} is a short story about an unknown group of entities searching for what makes a common man different from all others. It is a fantasy action thriller looking into a subject long ignored.

{ALONE A WAY OF LIFE} IS A SHORT STORY of a man who has decided he would rather live his life away from society. But he is thrust into a life or death encounter that may just change his mind.

{CHRISTMAS, IS NOT JUST ANOTHER DAY} is a short story in modern times but with a timeless message of love and spirit.

{VIRUS PANDEMIC} is a short story of possibilities. Was this a Chinese plot to gain control of the world or just a freak accident as they have claimed. The reader is left to decide.

Made in the USA
Middletown, DE
31 October 2024

63123236R00043